First Facts

Your Favorite Authors

JEFF Kinney

by Kelli L. Hicks

CAPSTONE PRESS
a capstone imprint

First Facts are published by Capstone Press,
1710 Roe Crest Drive, North Mankato, Minnesota 56003
www.capstonepub.com

Library of Congress Cataloging-in-Publication Data
Hicks, Kelli L.
   Jeff Kinney / by Kelli L. Hicks.
      pages cm.—(First Facts. Your Favorite Authors)
   Includes bibliographical references and index.
   Summary: "Presents the life and career of Jeff Kinney, including his childhood, education,
and milestones as a best-selling children's author"—Provided by publisher.
   ISBN 978-1-4765-0222-9 (library binding)
   ISBN 978-1-4765-3437-4 (paperback)
   ISBN 978-1-4765-3419-0 (eBook PDF)
   1. Kinney, Jeff—Juvenile literature. 2. Authors, American—21st century—Biography—
Juvenile literature. 3. Children's stories—Authorship—Juvenile literature. I. Title.
   PS3611.I634Z66 2014
   813'.6—dc23
   [B]   2013003119

Editorial Credits
Christopher L. Harbo, editor; Tracy Davies McCabe and Gene Bentdahl, designers;
Marcie Spence, media researcher; Kathy McColley, production specialist

Photo Credits
Alamy: Christina Kennedy, 17 (right), Jeff Morgan 05, 21 (left), Roi Brooks, 15 (right); AP
Images: Abrams Books for Young Readers, 13, Dave Aliocca, StarPix, 15 (left), Gretchen Ertl,
17 (left), PRNewsFoto/Skinit, Inc., 21 (right), The Buffalo News, Harry Scull Jr., 19 (top right);
Capstone: Michael Byers, cover, 9 (bottom); Capstone Studio: Karon Dubke, 11; Getty Images,
Inc.: G Flume, 9 (middle), Gail Oskin/WireImage for Macy's, 5; Newscom: Fox 2000 Pictures/
Pera, David Becker/UPI, 19 (bottom), Diyah, 7, ZUMA Press, 19 (top left); Shutterstock: ARENA
Creative, design element, Olga Tropinina, 9 (right), Sarah Kinnel, design element, strelov,
design element, Tania A, 7 (film); U.S. Air Force photo by Staff Sgt. Lee O. Tucker, 9 (top)

Printed in the United States of America in North Mankato, Minnesota.
032013   007223CGF13

Table of Contents

Chapter 1: An Author's Influence

In 2009 Jeff Kinney had a great year. First he won the Dorothy Canfield Fisher Children's Book Award. Then *Time* magazine picked Kinney as one of its 100 most **influential** people. Even better, Kinney's first book was being made into a movie. How did he make all of this happen? He wrote the *Diary of a Wimpy Kid* series.

---

influential—having the power to change or affect someone

"For me to imagine that I'm one of the 100 most influential people in the world is strange and wonderful, but also very silly. I'm not even the most influential person in my own house."—Jeff Kinney

Chapter 2: Where to Begin?

Jeff Kinney was born February 19, 1971, in Fort Washington, Maryland. He grew up with two brothers and one sister. His mom taught nursery school. His dad worked as a military **analyst**. It was his dad's love of newspaper comics that really changed Jeff's life. Every morning his dad would share the funny pages with Jeff.

---

analyst—someone who examines something carefully in order to understand it

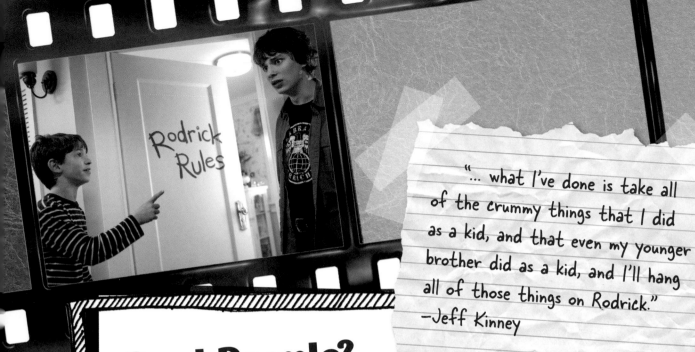

Real People?

Are Jeff and his brothers like any of the characters in his books? Jeff is a middle brother like his main character, Greg. Jeff's older brother did have a rock band, just like Greg's older brother, Rodrick. But Jeff says his characters are a mix of people he has known.

In 1989 Jeff **graduated** from Bishop McNamara High School in Forestville, Maryland. He planned to join the Air Force, but his love of comics changed his mind. He attended the University of Maryland with the dream of being a cartoonist. While there, he created the comic strip *Igdoof* for the campus newspaper. *Igdoof* followed the adventures of a college freshman.

---

graduate—to finish a course of study in school and receive a diploma

University of Maryland campus

9

After college Kinney tried to get a job drawing cartoons. But the newspapers he sent his drawings to **rejected** his cartoons. Luckily he also enjoyed working with computers. He got a job with a website called Funbrain. At Funbrain he created online games and activities for kids.

---

reject—to refuse to accept something, such as an idea, drawing, or book

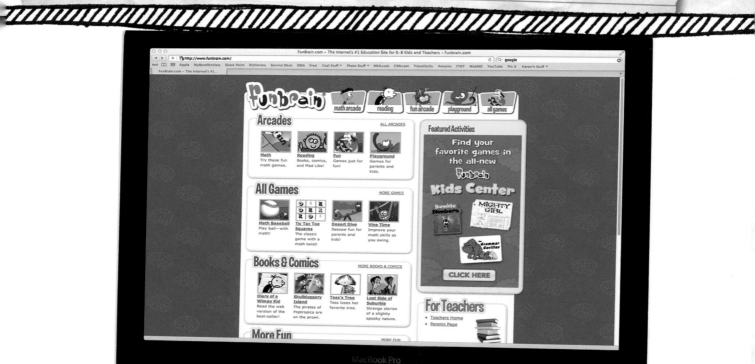

Chapter 3: Big Breaks

Kinney was not ready to give up cartoons. In 1998 he started working on a book called *Diary of a Wimpy Kid*. In 2004 he began posting sections of it daily on Funbrain's website. At first about 20,000 viewers a day visited the site. Soon more than 70,000 people a day viewed his work.

Kinney got his big break in 2006. During a comic book convention, he showed his book to an Abrams Books **editor**. The editor offered to **publish** Kinney's book for kids. *Diary of a Wimpy Kid* hit bookstores in April 2007. It soon became a *New York Times* best-seller. In time it rose to the number one spot.

---

editor—someone who checks the content of a book and gets it ready to be published

publish—to produce and distribute a book, magazine, or newspaper so that people can buy it

CRASH

SAN DIEGO
COMIC CON
INTERNATIONAL

COM
INTER
SAM

WWW.CO

New York
Times
best-seller!

DIARY
of a
Wimpy Kid

San Diego Comic Con

SCREECHHHHH

Kinney's success did not end with the first *Diary of a Wimpy Kid* book. Between 2008 and 2012, he published six more books in the series. He also published the *Diary of a Wimpy Kid Do-It-Yourself Book*. It teaches readers how to keep a journal. In 2010 *The Wimpy Kid Movie Diary* explained how Kinney's first book became a movie.

Diary of a Wimpy Kid jumped to the big screen in March 2010. The movie was a huge success. Two more movies quickly followed. *Diary of a Wimpy Kid: Rodrick Rules* opened in 2011. *Diary of a Wimpy Kid: Dog Days* hit theaters the next year. It includes events from the third and fourth *Diary of a Wimpy Kid* books.

Personal Side

Kinney lives in Plainville, Massachusetts. He and his wife, Julie, have two sons, Will and Grant.

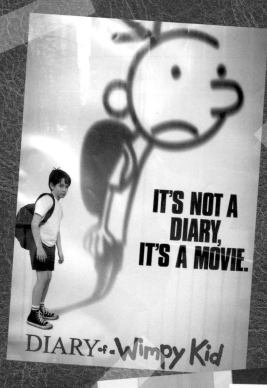

IT'S NOT A DIARY, IT'S A MOVIE.

DIARY of a Wimpy Kid

Kinney with Zachary Gordon, the actor who plays Greg

DOG DAYS

DIARY of a Wimpy Kid DOG DAYS

AUGUST 3

Chapter 4: Surprised by Success

Kinney's success surprises him. His books have been **translated** into 41 languages. More than 75 million copies are in print worldwide. Kinney plans to continue writing Wimpy Kid books. His eager fans can't wait to find out what happens next.

---

translate—to change one language into a different one

Poptropica

Kinney isn't just a successful author. In 2007 he created Poptropica.com, a gaming website for kids. On the site kids can create "Poptropican" characters. These characters explore stories, games, and go on adventures to the Islands of Poptropica.

Timeline

1971   born February 19 on an Air Force base in Maryland

1989   graduates from Bishop McNamara High School in Forestville, Maryland

2004   posts portions of *Diary of a Wimpy Kid* on the Funbrain website

2007   *Diary of a Wimpy Kid* is published

2008   *Diary of a Wimpy Kid: Rodrick Rules* is published

2009   *Diary of a Wimpy Kid: The Last Straw* and *Diary of a Wimpy Kid: Dog Days* are published; named to *Time* magazine's Most Influential People list; wins Dorothy Canfield Fisher Children's Book Award

2010   *The Wimpy Kid Movie Diary* and *Diary of a Wimpy Kid: The Ugly Truth* are published; the movie *Diary of a Wimpy Kid* is released

2011   the movie *Diary of a Wimpy Kid: Rodrick Rules* is released; *Diary of a Wimpy Kid: Cabin Fever* is published

2012   the movie *Diary of a Wimpy Kid: Dog Days* is released; *Diary of a Wimpy Kid: The Third Wheel* is published

2013   the *Diary of a Wimpy Kid* series is nominated for a Nickelodeon Kids' Choice Award

Glossary

analyst (AN-uhl-ist)—someone who examines something carefully in order to understand it

editor (ED-uh-tur)—someone who checks the content of a book and gets it ready to be published

graduate (GRAJ-oo-ate)—to finish a course of study in school and receive a diploma

influential (in-floo-EN-shul)—having the power to change or affect someone

publish (PUHB-lish)—to produce and distribute a book, magazine, or newspaper so that people can buy it

reject (ri-JEKT)—to refuse to accept something, such as an idea, drawing, or book

translate (TRANS-late)—to change one language into a different one

Read More

Corbett, Sue. *Jeff Kinney.* Spotlight on Children's Authors. New York: Marshall Cavendish Benchmark, 2013.

Webster, Christine, and Karen Durrie. *Jeff Kinney.* Remarkable Writers. New York: AV2 by Weigl, 2013.

Internet Sites

FactHound offers a safe, fun way to find Internet sites related to this book. All of the sites on FactHound have been researched by our staff.

Here's all you do:

Visit *www.facthound.com*

Type in this code: 9781476502229

Index

awards, 4, 22

birth, 6, 22
books, 4, 7, 12, 14, 16, 18, 20, 22

comic strips, 6, 8

education, 8, 22

family, 6, 7, 18
Funbrain, 10, 12, 22

movies, 4, 16, 18, 22

Poptropica, 21

Super-cool stuff!

Check out projects, games and lots more at
www.capstonekids.com